AF483237

My Dream, My Destiny

"Great Rewards come to those who Overcome Obstacles"

By Mahendra jagir

Dedication

I, Mahendra Jagir, the writer of this book, and my grandson, Matthew, who owns the title of this book, *MY DREAM, MY DESTINY*, want to dedicate this book to Matthew's twin brother, Dustin.

My wife Ajit, our family friend Sara, and I took care of Dustin and taught him many different activities and subjects using a chalkboard. It was quite a challenging task. At the age of 3, Dustin was able to remember all the planets in the solar system, along with math, reading, complex shapes, and much more.

In the middle of all this, something astonishing happened. Matthew, who was just a 3-year-old toddler, inspired me, a 72-year-old grandpa, to write this book. On 2/24/21, during our regular study time, Matthew said, *MY DREAM, MY DESTINY* nine times in a row. He also knew the alphabet and vowels in multiple languages like English, Greek, Spanish, French, Russian, and even some Mandarin, even though we don't speak these languages at home.

Matthew's words had such a strong impact on me that they motivated me to write my own book about my dream and my destiny. That's why I decided to name this book, *MY DREAM, MY DESTINY*.

From the last flight of Mahendra Jagir – March 17th, 2024

Acknowledgment

First and foremost, my praises and thanks to the God, the Almighty, for His Guidance and Blessings for making my journey of life possible.

Secondly, I would like to express my deep and sincere thanks to my mom, Channo, and my dad, Jagir, who, after going through many adversities in life, migrated from India to Fiji and beyond to give me a chance at life and make everything possible. My special thanks to my favorite grandmother, Mai Ishri, whose blessings and love protected me from many dangers in life.

My heartfelt thanks to my wife Ajit, who supported and made my family possible. My many thanks to my sons Michael and Rocky who kept me on my toes and making me very proud throughout their education and career achievements.

Next, my many thanks to my brothers and sisters-in-law, and my sisters and brothers-in-law, for mentoring and supporting me throughout my life.

Many thanks to my daughters-in-law for extending our family by blessing us with grandchildren, who kept us entertained and smiling.

My special thanks to Carter Flygare, Certified Flight Instructor, now a Chief Pilot in Sacramento Region, for training and instilling values in me to become the most daring pilot ever.

Many thanks to my friends and relatives across the world who kept me entertained and smiling.

Last but not least, my heartfelt "SPECIAL" thanks to my friends, publisher's, Ethan Hale and the team for making this book possible.

Like they say "it takes a village"

Thank you all!

Table of Contents

About the Author

Born in Fiji to the parents from India, the author envisions his dream of becoming a pilot one day.

This book is about the author who was born in Caubati, Suva, Fiji Islands. He was born to a family of 10 siblings beginning with his oldest sister Sibo, and his older brothers, Nashiv, Sansara, Gulzara, Hazara, Pyara, Joginder, and his younger brother Hardip, his little sister, Hardeep Kaur and his youngest brother, Gurmail. His half-sister, Bachno, was born in Punjab, India, stayed there with her family. She migrated to USA with her family in early 1973.

His dad was orphaned at age 5 when his father, Moti, Author's Grandfather, passed away with some unknown illness in India. Soon after his father's death, his mom, Chinti, author's grandmother, was returned to her village due to some stringent Punjabi customs applied to widows during those times.

As an orphan, he faced many adversities of life. He was raised by his Uncle Atra. He missed his mom very much. He had many hungry and sleepless nights throughout his life along with getting married twice before migrating to Fiji.

The author born in Fiji had his own set of adversities of life beginning with his birth.

His mission was to work hard and raise an educated family with resilience and to share their experiences with the world with dignity and human kindness.

He is a very strong believer of equality, meaning "no more, no less."

He believes in human kindness. "Help those who need care, employment, food, clothing and shelter to a point where they can get back on their feet and not become a public liability.

You have one shot at life!

"BE THE BEST, BE # 1"

He is your friend, Mahendra Jagir.

"GIVE BACK!"

Page Blank Intentionally

Preface

Within the following pages lies the remarkable chronicle of an individual who dared to chase his dreams against all odds. This narrative is not merely a recounting of personal triumphs but a celebration of the indomitable human spirit, which knows no bounds when fueled by passion and tenacity.

The story you are about to discover weaves through the fabric of one man's life—a life colored by moments of adversity, perseverance, and ultimately, fulfillment. From humble beginnings etched with struggle and uncertainty to the realization of a seemingly improbable childhood aspiration, this journey resonates with the essence of resilience and the pursuit of one's true calling.

Through the highs and lows of his odyssey, our protagonist navigates challenges that might have deterred the faint-hearted. Yet, with unwavering resolve and a steadfast belief in his vision, he presses on, proving that with determination, anything is possible.

As you immerse yourself in the narrative that unfolds, may you find inspiration in the protagonist's unwavering commitment to his dreams. May you be reminded that the human spirit is capable of transcending barriers and overcoming obstacles, no matter how daunting they may seem.

Chapter 1

"Life is like a box of chocolates" as Forest Gump so eloquently put it. You never quite know what you're going to get. And for my family, our box of chocolates was filled with a myriad of flavors—some bitter, some sweet, but all contributing to the rich tapestry of our journey.

It all began when my parents, born and raised in the heart of Punjab, India, set foot on the shores of Fiji in the early 1930s. Their roots, firmly embedded in the soil of their homeland, intertwined with the promise of new beginnings in a distant land. My father, Jagir, born in the Village, Herian, in 1909 and my mother, Channo, born in the Village, Jabbowal, in 1917, brought with them a legacy of resilience, forged in the crucible of adversity.

My father's childhood was marked by hardship from the very start. Orphaned at the tender age of five, he was raised by his uncle and aunt. His widowed mom, Chinti Bhutta, from Village Barra Dosanja, was sealed by the customs of that time. She was, deprived, despised, and excluded from the family. She was sent back to her village. Separated from his mother, he toiled away...But adversity only served to fuel his determination. With each sunrise, he labored tirelessly, saving every penny in the pursuit of a better tomorrow. At the age of sixteen, guided by the traditions of his culture, he entered into an arranged marriage—a union that would shape the course of his life in ways he could never have imagined.

His first wife, my aunt, bore him a daughter before tragically passing away just three years later. Faced with the responsibility of providing for his child, my father found himself once again at a crossroads. And it was my mother, his first wife's youngest sister, that he found solace and strength.

Their union, born out of necessity, soon blossomed into a love that transcended the trials of life.

But the call of opportunity beckoned by his cousin, Rakha Ram, who was already in Fiji, advised my dad to join him. In the early 1930s, my parents made the courageous decision to leave behind the familiar comforts of home and seek a brighter future in Fiji. Their journey, fraught with uncertainty and peril, mirrored the turbulent seas upon which they sailed.

From the crowded and buzzing streets of a small city in Punjab, to the crowded decks of a ship bound for Fiji, their path was marked by trials and tribulations. Three harrowing days on a train from Punjab to Calcutta, followed by a perilous voyage across the ocean, saw them endure hardships that tested the very limits of their endurance. Yet, fueled by the promise of a better tomorrow, they pressed onward, their spirits undaunted by the challenges that lay ahead.

Their first stop was in Singapore and then to Malaysia. Malaysia offered a brief respite, a chance to replenish their supplies and gather their strength for the journey ahead. From there, they continued on to Perth, Australia, where the ship was serviced and loaded with provisions once more. The voyage stretched on, with stops in Adelaide, Melbourne, and Sydney, each port a fleeting glimpse of a world beyond the horizon.

Yet, amidst the endless expanse of the ocean, the journey was not without its perils. Many succumbed to seasickness, their dreams dimmed by the relentless swell of the waves. But my parents, buoyed by their unwavering resolve, pressed on, their eyes fixed on the distant shores of their new home.

Finally, after two months at sea, their ship docked in Suva, Fiji Islands, a beacon of hope amidst the vastness of the Pacific Ocean.

Their journey began with humble beginnings, as they worked the sugarcane plantations, their hands calloused from the labor of the land. But with each drop of sweat shed beneath the scorching sun, they nurtured the seeds of ambition, dreaming of a future filled with promise and prosperity.

It was through sheer hard work and relentless dedication that they were able to purchase their first farming property in Caubati, Suva. There, amidst the verdant fields, they cultivated a livelihood, growing vegetables and root plants that they sold in the marketplace. It was a labor of love, a testament to their unwavering resolve to build a better future for their growing family.

As the years passed, their efforts bore fruit, both literally and figuratively. My oldest sister, "Sibo" was born, a testament to the blessings that their newfound prosperity bestowed upon them. Yet, even as they celebrated the joys of parenthood, my parents never wavered in their pursuit of the American dream.

In the 1940s, my father learned of an opportunity for his children to migrate to the United States. He wasted no time in registering the first three newborns with the American Embassy, laying the groundwork for a future filled with promise and possibility.

Meanwhile, life continued to unfold, and our family expanded with the arrival of more children. But amidst the joys of parenthood, there were responsibilities to be fulfilled. My half-sister "Bachno," now fifteen, was ready to embark on her own journey into adulthood. And so, in 1949, my mother made the arduous journey back to India to oversee her marriage.

It was a journey marked by hardship and sacrifice, as my mother navigated the complexities of arranging a marriage while pregnant with my older brother. Yet, despite the challenges, she remained steadfast in her determination to ensure the well-being of her family.

Two years passed before my mother returned to Fiji, her toddler son, Joginder "Joe" in tow, a testament to her unwavering love and dedication. The journey back was fraught with challenges, as my brother fell ill several times en route. But through it all, my mother remained a pillar of strength, her love guiding us safely back home.

Now, here's where all the "drama" began…

April 9th, 1952.

The sun beat down relentlessly on the farms of Fiji, and my mom, heavily pregnant with me, was in the thick of it all. Despite the scorching heat, she felt strangely energetic that day, as if nothing could dampen her spirits. But then, as she worked in the fields, labor pains hit her like a ton of bricks.

She knew something was up when her water broke. So, she rushed home, hoping the nearby midwives could help. Can you believe it? Nine midwives tried, but none could deliver me. Talk about a tough day at the office!

With no other options, my dad sprang into action. Without phones to call for help, he mounted his trusty steed—a horse—and rode like the wind to the "Kings Road, which was 4.5 miles away from Suva. There, he tied his horse at the neighbor's yard, with their permission, and rode the bus to the Colonial War Memorial Hospital (CWM). Imagine that scene: my dad, racing against time on horseback to save the day. At the hospital, he pleaded for assistance, and they sent him back with Dr. Al

Mendel, a traveling gynecologist. They arrived back home in style, in a cab, with Dr. Mendel in tow. But the journey wasn't over yet. They still had to ride that horse up to our house from the main highway!

By the time they got there, my mom was probably a nervous wreck. But Dr. Mendel wasted no time. And just like that, I made my grand entrance into the world.

Born naturally, weighing in at a whopping 12 pounds and 13 ounces, my arrival into the world was no small feat. The complications of my birth were evident from the start, but despite the challenges, my mom and I emerged unscathed—a testament to our resilience.

My dad, ever the resourceful one, paid the doctor "Three Sterling Pounds" (That's six dollars today) for his services, a bargain considering the circumstances. And as I took my first breaths of fresh air, I couldn't help but feel relieved to have made it through the ordeal in one piece.

Life on the prevailing trade wind side of Viti Levu, the largest of 332 islands of Fiji, was no walk in the park. It covers about 57% of the nation's land area and hosts the capital city, Suva. The climate varies significantly from east to west. The mountain range divides Viti Levi climatically into a wet southeastern section 120 inches of rain annually and a dry northwestern section 70–90 inches. It falls on Coordinates: 17°48′S 178°0′E. With frequent rain and perpetually muddy ground, every day brought its own set of challenges. Yet, amidst the adversity, my parents had a vision—a plan to secure our future.

They invested in three parcels of farmland, each boasting about six acres of fertile soil. On each "parcel" of land my dad built a house, laying the groundwork for a future where his children would settle down and thrive. It was a grand plan, one filled with hope and optimism for the generations to come.

***

As time ticked on, my oldest sister, who had been like a second mother to me during my infancy, was now 17. It was a milestone moment, a time when tradition dictated that she should embark on the journey of marriage. Despite being born and raised in Fiji, as i mentioned earlier, it was customary for girls to be wed in India through arranged marriages.

So, in accordance with this tradition, my father escorted her to India, where he had meticulously arranged a match with a highly-educated young man. With her future secured, my sister began her own family in India before eventually migrating to England several years later and United States afterwards.

Meanwhile, back in Fiji, my father continued to nurture our family's land, a labor of love that extended beyond our own needs. Of the three parcels he had purchased, we lived on one and worked the fields of all three. But my father's generosity knew no bounds. He opened the doors of the other two homes to friends and relatives in need, providing them with not just shelter, but also an acre of land to cultivate and sustain themselves.

Life on our farm was simple yet challenging. With no running water or electricity, we relied on kerosene lamps to illuminate our homes and gathered firewood for cooking and heating. Washing clothes in the nearby stream and ironing them with iron that required heated charcoal were just part of our daily routine.

I'll admit, as a teenager, I often pestered my father about moving to the city for a better life. But he would just smile and promise that one day, our time would come. And although the allure of city comforts tantalized me, looking back, I realize that it was on that humble farm, surrounded by family and fueled by my father's unwavering optimism, that I learned the true value of resilience and community.

Our days were filled with the rhythm of farm life—planting, tending, harvesting, and selling our crops at the bustling marketplace in the city. From crisp cabbage to tender beans, and from hearty taro to starchy cassava, we cultivated a bounty of vegetables and root plants to sustain our family and earn a living.

But farming wasn't just a livelihood; it was a way of life. Each member of our family had their assigned chores, and even at the tender age of six, I had mine—to milk the cows before and after school. I can still recall vividly the first time I attempted this task. With determination in my heart and a bucket in hand, I approached the cow, tying her down to a stump as I had been taught. Yet, halfway through, disaster struck—the cow kicked the bucket full of milk.

Disheartened, I returned home with an empty bucket, only to face my mom's disappointment at not being able to enjoy her tea "with" milk. But undeterred, I approached the second cow, who seemed to offer a reassuring smile. This time, I completed the task without incident, bringing home a bucket brimming with milk and a sense of accomplishment.

From that day forward, I never faltered in my duties. The lesson was clear—persistence pays off. "Where there is a will, there is a way," as the saying goes. And so, life on the farm continued, punctuated by the births of "my brother Hardip (Boss), my little sister, Hardeep, and my youngest brother Gurmail (Bob)," to continue with the rhythm of our chores.

Despite the challenges of farm life, my parents' dreams for our future burned brightly. They toiled tirelessly to ensure we received a quality education, with my mom setting high expectations for academic excellence. Her own lack of formal education only fueled her determination to see us succeed, instilling in us the values of hard work and perseverance that would guide us through life's challenges.

In the year 1960, a significant opportunity knocked on the doors of our family in Fiji. It was the American Embassy, extending an invitation to my three oldest brothers through the "Quota System" to make a life-changing journey to the United States. Without hesitation, they seized the chance, each stepping forward to apply for their immigration visas.

In a matter of days, their visas were granted, paving the way for their migration to the land of opportunity. Booking cabins on the famed ships of P & O Orient Lines—Oriana, Oronsay, or Arcadia—they embarked on a journey across the Pacific, bound for the golden shores of San Francisco, California.

Upon arrival, armed with their farming skills and a determination to succeed, they sought out opportunities in Northern California, particularly in Yuba City. They found work on farms, laboring tirelessly to pick peaches, pears, plums, and to tend to the orchards through pruning seasons. Their hard work paid off, and after a few years, they transitioned to jobs in Sacramento, finding employment on golf courses.

Back in Fiji, the rest of our family carried on with our lives. We attended school diligently, lending our hands to assist our parents in the daily toils of farming. Our parents' tales of struggle served as a constant reminder that nothing worth having comes easy. We "imbibed" their teachings, pouring our efforts into our studies and work, refusing to yield to adversity.

I owe a debt of gratitude to my parents, who embarked on a perilous journey from India to Fiji in search of a better life for their children. Their sacrifices and unwavering determination laid the foundation for our future, enabling us to pursue even greater opportunities in the United States.

Chapter 2

February 18, 1957, was a day etched in my memory, the day when the skies above Suva, Fiji Islands, erupted with a deafening roar. At just five years old, I was playing with my friends on the school grounds when the sound of three planes flying in formation shattered the tranquility of the afternoon. I couldn't help but be captivated by the sight, my young mind buzzing with curiosity and wonder.

Approaching my teacher with wide-eyed innocence, I sought an explanation for this aerial spectacle. With a patient smile, she enlightened me, revealing that these planes were probably part "of the Royal Air Force (RAF) based out of Australia practicing and protecting their colonies by flying in synchronized form." Though my understanding was limited, the notion of these mighty machines soaring through the skies left an indelible impression on my young mind.

From that moment on, I found myself gazing skyward with renewed fervor, hoping to catch another glimpse of these flying marvels. Yet, sightings of planes were rare in those days, with sea travel reigning supreme for shipping and transportation.

But even as I continued my education, diligently attending school and assisting my family on the farms, the allure of the skies lingered in the back of my mind. It wasn't until my brother Jack became a US citizen and petitioned for our family to migrate to the United States in 1968 that the possibility of becoming a pilot began to feel within reach.

With our immigrant visa secured in early February 1968, the prospect of a new beginning beckoned, offering the promise of fulfilling dreams once thought unattainable. And as I embarked on this new chapter of my journey, the echoes of those planes soaring overhead served as a poignant reminder of the boundless opportunities awaiting us in the land of the free.

On March 17, 1968, a new chapter of our lives began as my mom, my little sister Muni, my little brother Babu, and I embarked on a journey across the Pacific Ocean bound for California, USA. Our vessel, the "Oriana," a majestic cruise ship operated by the renowned P&O Orient Lines, served as our floating home for the next thirteen days.

Our first port of call was the vibrant city of Honolulu, Hawaii, where we arrived on March 23, 1968. But before we could set foot on Hawaiian soil, our ship was intercepted at sea by the Coast Guard, who meticulously verified and stamped our visa and medical records, officially granting us legal status as residents of the United States. Honolulu served as our gateway to the USA, and as we approached the port, a towering structure shaped like a pineapple greeted us—a symbol of the island's tropical allure.

During our brief stay in Honolulu, I seized the opportunity to explore the city through an organized bus tour. Stepping off the ship, we were met with our first taste of cultural shock—the escalator, a marvel of modern technology that whisked us down to street level with ease. Observing the locals, we quickly learned the ropes and descended without mishap, boarding the tour bus that would take us on a journey through downtown Honolulu.

The bustling city streets, skyscrapers towering overhead, and the cacophony of traffic were a stark contrast to the tranquil landscapes of Fiji. Yet, we adapted swiftly, immersing ourselves in the sights and sounds of our new surroundings. As the tour bus ventured into the rural outskirts of the city, we marveled at the vast expanses of pineapple and sugar cane plantations stretching as far as the eye could see—a sight that left us in awe, especially considering that the entire area of all the islands of Fiji amounted to a mere fraction of the state of California.

It was a journey of discovery, a glimpse into a world vastly different from our own, but one that we embraced with open arms. And as we continued our voyage towards California, the promise of new adventures and opportunities beckoned, filling our hearts with excitement and anticipation for the journey that lay ahead. Top of Form

***

Becoming legal American residents was a milestone in our journey, marking the beginning of a new chapter filled with both excitement and challenges. At fifteen years old, I found myself thrust into the role of decision-maker, navigating unfamiliar territory with a mixture of apprehension and determination. Thankfully, my schooling in geography proved invaluable, providing a foundation that eased our travels and helped me navigate the unknown.

As our bus tour came to an end, we returned to the ship, ready to continue our voyage towards Vancouver, Canada. Three days at sea brought us to the approach of Vancouver's bustling port, where the iconic Lions Gate Bridge awaited us. Standing on the upper deck, we marveled at the sight, the bridge looming overhead as our ship passed gracefully beneath it—an exhilarating moment etched into my memory.

Arriving in Vancouver, we had twelve hours to explore the city while the ship unloaded passengers bound for Canada. With a transit pass in hand, courtesy of the ship, I seized the opportunity to join friends and relatives in discovering the charms of Vancouver. "A relative named Sadhu. His parents had family ties with my parents. We regularly met each other at

Temple gatherings." He invited us to join his brother and his family for a tour of the city, and we eagerly accepted.

Welcomed into their home, we were treated to a feast of homemade delights, the flavors of which linger in my memory to this day. Energized by our meal, we set out to explore Vancouver, visiting museums and taking in the sights of this vibrant city. It was a day of discovery and camaraderie, culminating in a timely return to the ship as we set sail once more, bound for our final destination—San Francisco, California.

The three-day journey to San Francisco was filled with anticipation, each passing moment bringing us closer to the next chapter of our adventure in the land of opportunity. As we approached the iconic Golden Gate Bridge, the anticipation of our arrival in San Francisco grew palpable. Passing through the narrow opening to San Francisco Bay and under the majestic bridge, I was greeted by a breathtaking panorama of skyscrapers, bustling boats of all shapes and sizes, and the mesmerizing sight of planes soaring overhead. In that moment, amidst the hustle and bustle of the bay, I felt a stirring of excitement and the realization that my dream of becoming a private pilot was well within reach.

Finally, on April 1st, 1968, our voyage culminated as we arrived at our final destination in San Francisco, California. With a mix of anticipation and apprehension, I ventured out to see if anyone had come to greet us, mindful of the date—April Fools' Day. The thought crossed my mind that my brothers might mistake our arrival for a prank, but as I stepped onto the bustling streets of San Francisco, I was filled with hope and excitement.

Stepping off the ship onto the bustling port of San Francisco, I scanned the crowd anxiously, searching for any familiar faces. And there he was—my oldest brother, “Chand,” marching up and down the dock in a frenzy of excitement. Spotting me, he nearly burst with joy, calling out my name in a mixture of relief and exhilaration. I couldn’t help but smile as I waved him off, assuring him that I had everything under control.

Returning to my family waiting in the cabin, I relayed the good news, easing their worries as we prepared to disembark. Loading our baggage onto a cart, we made our way down to the lower deck, where our family awaited with open arms. Tears of joy flowed freely as we embraced, grateful for our safe arrival.

With our belongings loaded into their cars, we set off towards Sacramento, the wide, straight freeways stretching out before us. Amazed by the sheer size of the roads, I couldn’t help but share my idea with my brother Jack—a solution to the “madness” of driving on such straight paths. Proposing the idea of magnetic tape to guide the cars, I was met with laughter and disbelief, a reminder that I was still adjusting to life in this new land.

Arriving in Sacramento, we settled into our new home—a modest three-bedroom house with a garage. Despite the cramped quarters, I relished the newfound luxuries of electricity and privacy. My room in the garage became my sanctuary, a place where I could study and unwind in peace. And as I settled in Sacramento, I couldn’t help but feel a sense of gratitude for my brother’s generosity.

***

Despite the challenges of being thrust into a new environment, my brother wasted no time in registering me at Hiram Johnson High School, handing me the responsibility of finding my own way home—an unexpected test of my independence. With limited knowledge of my surroundings, I navigated the streets of Sacramento with determination and a touch of uncertainty.

You see, in those days, communication was primitive compared to today's standards—no cell phones, just dial phones and the occasional telegram. Yet, amidst the simplicity of the times, there was a sense of safety and community that permeated our daily lives. I quickly learned to adapt, making friends like Leonard Brown, who helped me navigate the intricacies of the school bus system and find my way home safely.

My brother Jack played a pivotal role in my transition to life in the United States, serving as both mentor and teacher. As a Golf Course Superintendent at El Macero Country Club, he imparted valuable lessons not only in golf but also in life, instilling in me a strong work ethic and a passion for excellence. Under his guidance, I learned the intricacies of golf course maintenance and developed a love for the sport that would stay with me throughout my life.

As I settled into my new school routine, I quickly realized that chaos reigned supreme in the classroom. Kids were slouching with their feet up, chewing gum like it was going out of style, and launching paper planes like they were fighter jets. And let me tell you, as someone who dreamed of soaring the skies as a pilot, it was a pretty disappointing sight.

Coming from a background where discipline was as ingrained as tying your shoelaces, this lack of order was downright shocking. Back in Fiji, we wore school uniforms and sat with our arms folded, hanging on every word the teacher said.

But here, it seemed like anything went. I couldn't sit idly by and watch it happen, so I took matters into my own hands. I marched straight to my counselor's office and poured out my frustrations. To her credit, she didn't brush me off. Instead, she challenged me to take action.

So, I put pen to paper and poured my heart into a three-page article, outlining the need for more discipline in our school. I didn't just point out the problems—I offered solutions, too. And you know what? They listened. My article made waves, and soon enough, it was published in the school paper with high praise.

But the story didn't end there. The school board took notice and promised to address the issue at their next meeting. And guess what? They actually followed through! They adopted stricter discipline rules, paving the way for a better learning environment for all.

It was a small victory, but it felt like a triumph for all of us who believed in the power of structure and order.

***

Ah, the excitement of freedom after graduating high school! With my shiny new driver's license in hand, I felt like the world was at my fingertips. But there was one dream that tugged at my heartstrings more than anything else: flying planes.

So, during my first semester at Sacramento City College, I met a fellow student named John in my Psychology class. We hit it off, and before long, we were thick as thieves. One day, I couldn't contain my excitement any longer, so I asked John if he'd ever been up in the air before. When he said no, I knew what we had to do.

We hatched a plan to ditch school for a day and head to Sacramento Metropolitan Airport to make our flying dreams a reality. As we approached the PSA (Pacific Southwest Airlines) counter, I could feel my heart racing with anticipation. I boldly asked the representative if we could fly to San Francisco and back, just for fun.

To my surprise, he didn't bat an eyelid. He simply nodded and quoted us a price of $18.00 per person—a small fortune for a couple of college students scraping by on part-time wages. But the thrill of the adventure outweighed any financial concerns.

With our reservations secured, we eagerly awaited our flight. PSA Flight #18 would whisk us away to San Francisco at 10:35 am, promising an exhilarating journey through the clouds. And if that wasn't enough, we'd be back in Sacramento by 2:10 pm, courtesy of PSA Flight #19.

The thrill of takeoff is something I'll never forget. The roar of the engines, the rush of acceleration—it was like nothing I'd ever experienced before. As we soared through the sky, I couldn't tear my eyes away from the window, watching the world below shrink into tiny dots.

Touching down in San Francisco, I was struck by the sheer scale of the airport. Rows upon rows of planes, each one destined for a different corner of the globe. It was a mesmerizing sight, and I couldn't help but feel a surge of excitement coursing through my veins.

But our adventure wasn't over yet. After a quick sandwich, it was time to head back home. Boarding PSA Flight #19, I felt a sense of pride knowing that I was embarking on yet another step towards my dream of becoming a pilot.

In 1970, I stumbled upon another opportunity to indulge my passion for flying—this time, with a friend named Ajit, who would become my wife in 10 years." She was less than enthusiastic about taking to the skies. But curiosity got the better of her, and soon we found ourselves at a glider plane airport in Vacaville.

Watching the gliders take off and land was a sight to behold. The way they soared effortlessly through the air, catching thermals and riding the wind—it was like poetry in motion. And when the opportunity arose for us to take a ride ourselves, we didn't hesitate.

Strapped into our seats, we soared through the sky with our hearts in our throats. Our pilot was a daredevil, swooping and diving with the grace of a bird in flight. It was exhilarating, terrifying, and utterly unforgettable.

But amidst the adrenaline and excitement, one thing became clear: my passion for flying was stronger than ever. And so, armed with newfound confidence and determination, I set out on a mission to turn my childhood dream into a reality.

Summer of 1970 found me at Sacramento Executive Airport, eager to learn more about what it would take to become a "pilot". At Executive Flyers flight school, I was met with encouraging words and a clear path forward. The cost may have seemed steep, but for me, it was a small price to pay for the chance to chase my dreams.

Feeling the rush of adrenaline from my previous flights, my determination to become a pilot soared even higher. In the summer of 1970, I decided to take my quest to the next level and visited the Sacramento Executive Airport to explore the requirements and costs involved in realizing my childhood dream.

At Executive Flyers flight school, the staff welcomed me warmly and listened intently as I poured out my passion for flying. When they quoted the cost of approximately $700.00 to obtain my pilot's license, my heart sank. It was a sum beyond my means at the time.

But just as I was about to turn away, defeated, they offered me a lifeline—a chance to try their flight simulator. Without hesitation, I dove in, embracing the opportunity to immerse myself in the world of aviation. With each simulated takeoff and landing, I felt as though I was soaring through the clouds, my spirit lifted by the promise of what could be.

As I reluctantly left the flight school that day, I thanked them for the unforgettable experience and vowed to return one day, when my pockets were a little deeper. Their encouragement echoed in my ears, reminding me that my dream of becoming a pilot was within reach, even if it required patience and perseverance to achieve.

And the Drama Continues...

In June 1973, I proudly received my AA Degree in General Education from Sacramento City College, marking the beginning of my academic journey. But my passion for aviation continued to burn bright, urging me to pursue my dream of becoming a pilot.

Undeterred by the demands of higher education, I enrolled at California State University, Sacramento, where I delved deeper into my studies. In 1976, I proudly walked across the stage to accept my Bachelor's Degree in Sociology/Psychology, a testament to my dedication and perseverance. Fuelled by ambition, I pressed on, setting my sights on a Master's Degree in the same field.

By 1978, I had completed all the requirements for my Master's Degree, save for the elusive Master's Thesis. Though I never crossed that final hurdle, my academic journey had enriched me in countless ways. And as life unfolded, I embarked on a new chapter—I got married in 1980.

With my wife, Ajit by my side, we welcomed two sons into our family, Michael and Rocky. Together, we dedicated ourselves to serving our community through a federally funded program, a non-profit organization committed to providing vital social services to underprivileged communities.

In my role as Coordinator for the Sacramento Downtown Community Service Center, I worked tirelessly to support the needs of our low-income residents. From screening and monitoring to facilitating essential referrals, I ensured that help reached those who needed it most. As a youth coordinator, I took pride in organizing after-school lunch programs and engaging activities for disadvantaged youth, fostering a sense of belonging and opportunity in their lives.

With the program's support, I orchestrated soccer and baseball teams, as well as enriching field trips, empowering our youth to thrive despite their challenging circumstances. It was more than a job—it was a calling, a chance to make a tangible difference in the lives of those who needed it most.

The year 1980 brought unexpected challenges as the Federal Government Program I had dedicated myself to ran out of funds, leaving me without a job. However, I refused to let adversity define me. Instead, I embraced the opportunity for new experiences.

I delved into the world of real estate, navigating the complicated world of property transactions with diligence and determination. At the same time, I found myself drawn into the world of legal proceedings, serving as a court interpreter for the Yolo County Court. From EDD-unemployment appeals to Social

Security Disability Appeals and Medical Appeals, I found myself immersed in the intricacies of the legal system.

Remarkably, my efforts did not go unnoticed. The judges overseeing these proceedings recognized the value I brought to the courtroom with my precise interpretations and deep understanding of the law. In fact, they were so impressed that they expressed a desire to hire me permanently. But as Fate would have it, financial issues prevented them from doing so.

Yet, despite the uncertainty, I did my best to take every challenge head-on.

In 1983, something unexpected happened while I was hanging out at my friend's Chevron Station. I met Vern Driffil, a Chevron rep, and we hit it off. He thought I had what it takes to be a great businessman, so he pitched me an idea: become a Chevron Dealer.

I was curious, so I asked Vern what it all entailed. He said I'd need to do two weeks of training and sign a lease for six years. Oh, and there was a closed Chevron Station up for grabs right then and there.

I liked what I heard, so I went for it. No lawyers involved; just a handshake and trust. Vern gave me some solid advice, like running the business solo and not mixing business with family or friends.

After my training, I opened shop on February 18th, 1983. But business was slow at first. So, I got creative with marketing, putting up banners and handing out flyers to let people know we were back in business.

My brother, Bob, and nephew, John, were a huge help in those early days. They pitched in with everything from pumping gas to basic car repairs. And let's not forget about the toolbox my older brother Joe gave me. It's been a lifesaver. Those early days were tough, but with support from family and Vern's advice, I got through them. Little did I know, Chevron Station would be the start of my journey as an entrepreneur.

Those tools from my brother Joe were a game-changer. I mean, they helped kickstart my car repair business in a big way. I still remember our very first sale like it was yesterday. A guy rolls up needing a new battery, and I'm standing there scratching my head. Lucky for me, my mechanically gifted little brother was there to save the day and install it.

After that, business started booming. I got creative with marketing, organizing car wash fundraisers and all sorts of events to draw people in. And let me tell you, we had all kinds of customers – from locals to military personnel from McClellan Air Force Base, even pilots.

Speaking of pilots, they fascinated me. They'd swing by the station, and I'd pick their brains about flying. They'd tell me stories about their passion for soaring through the skies, defending the nation – it was captivating stuff. The more I learned, the more I was hooked. I knew I had to become a pilot myself someday.

Running the Chevron station was no walk in the park, though. I did everything from scrubbing toilets to managing the whole shebang. I only had one full-time mechanic, a guy named John, who was a real pro. We did everything from auto repairs to pumping gas for "Full Service" customers. And let me tell you, those old-school gas stations required a lot of manual work – processing credit cards, counting cash, the works.

I worked my tail off, from dawn 'til dusk, seven days a week, for six years straight. It was tough, especially balancing work with family life. I missed out on a lot of my kids' childhoods, and that's something I'll always regret. But back then, I was laser-focused on making the business a success.

I saw that opportunity with the Chevron station and grabbed it with both hands. It was all about providing for my family, you know? When the ground lease expired in '89, I shifted gears and invested in a couple of rental properties. That extra income was a game-changer – it meant we could afford better schools and cover all the costs without relying on student loans. Debt-free was the goal, and I'm proud to say we achieved it!

Chapter 3

October 1986.

It was quite a time! That's when I had a fascinating encounter with a solicitor named John. He swung by our place, spreading the word about his beliefs, and we got to chatting. Turns out, we shared a passion for hobbies – I was all about golf, and he was into flying planes.

Now, I didn't know much about planes back then, still getting my bearings, you know? But John mentioned he owned a sleek machine called a "Bonanza."

He swore it was faster than your average bird in the sky. I nodded along, trying to keep up with the airplane lingo. Little did I know, the Bonanza was a speed demon in the skies, with its low-wing design, V-tail, and shiny aluminum build, making it stand out from the crowd of wooden and fabric planes. It was like the Cadillac of aircraft, packed with all the bells and whistles for navigation.

Well, Saturday rolled around, and there I was, making my way to John's place down near Florin Road and Bradshaw Road in South Sacramento. As I pulled up, I couldn't believe my eyes. Right there in his backyard was this sleek, sporty Bonanza plane, tucked away in a hangar. And get this – he had his very own runway!

Now, picture this: an 800-foot dirt strip, right in his backyard, looking a bit uneven and bumpy. My nerves were on edge, to say the least, but I kept cool on the surface. After all, John seemed confident enough in his backyard flying skills. So, I took a deep breath and went along for the ride, trying not to let my paranoia get the best of me.

As we taxied out of John's backyard, the reality of what we were about to do hit me like a ton of bricks. Taking off from your own backyard? It felt like something out of a movie. But John, with his easy smile and confident demeanor, seemed unfazed. So I plastered on a brave face and tried to keep my nerves in check.

Once we were up in the air, though, it was like a whole new world opened up before us. The view was breathtaking, with the golden hues of Fall casting a warm glow over the landscape below. The air was crisp and clear, and for a moment, all my fears melted away. Flying high above the earth, I felt a sense of freedom unlike anything I'd ever experienced before.

Thirty minutes later, we touched down in Napa, ready for a delicious dinner at Jones's restaurant. But just as we were finishing up, fate threw us a curveball. A low tire and a dead battery? Talk about unexpected twists. My heart sank as I watched John deal with these issues, my mind racing with worst-case scenarios. But John, bless his heart, remained calm and collected, tackling each problem with a cool-headed determination that was nothing short of admirable.

As we prepared to head back, my nerves were on edge once again. The foggy evening only added to my sense of unease. But John's steady hand and unwavering confidence gave me hope. Even as we descended towards his backyard runway, with nothing but tree tops to guide us, I couldn't help but marvel at his skill and composure.

By the time I finally made it home, I felt like I'd aged a few years in just one evening. But as I stepped through the door and saw my family waiting for me, safe and sound, a wave of relief washed over me. Sure, that joy ride was one for the books, but there's something to be said for the simple comfort of home. And as I settled back into the familiar routines of everyday life, I couldn't help but feel a sense of gratitude for the little moments of peace and stability that anchor us in the storm. Bring on the next challenge, I thought. I was ready for whatever came my way.

And so, my next challenge came when I met "Bing."

Meeting Bing was like stumbling upon a hidden treasure. He was more than just a regular customer at my Chevron station; he was a kindred spirit, someone who shared my passion for flying. It didn't take long for us to strike up a friendship, chatting away about our dreams of soaring through the skies.

When Bing invited me to visit him at the Lincoln Airport, I jumped at the chance. I mean, who wouldn't want to hang out at an airport, right? Little did I know, that visit would change everything. As we wandered around the airport, Bing's enthusiasm for flying was infectious. And when he offered to take me for a ride in a Cessna 172 Skyhawk, I couldn't say 'yes' fast enough.

The thrill of that flight to Red Bluff is something I'll never forget. From the moment we took off to the smooth landing back at Lincoln Airport, I was hooked. Over lunch, as we chatted about flying and our shared dreams, I knew I had found my calling. It was like the pieces of the puzzle were finally falling into place.

By the time we touched down at Lincoln Airport, I was buzzing with excitement. I knew then and there that I wanted to pursue flight training, to turn my dream of becoming a pilot into reality. And with Bing by my side, guiding me every step of the way, I knew I had found the perfect mentor to help me reach my goals.

Soon, at the airport, I was introduced to a man who would become instrumental in my journey to becoming a pilot: Carter Flygare. Carter wasn't just a flight instructor; he was a seasoned aviator with a wealth of experience and a passion for teaching others how to fly. From the moment we met, Carter and I hit it off, bonding over our shared love of aviation and our life's adventures.

After some heartfelt conversations and getting to know each other better, Carter offered me a once-in-a-lifetime opportunity: a complimentary flight. Eager to seize the chance to experience flying from the pilot's seat, I eagerly accepted. As I climbed into my seat, a sense of exhilaration washed over me, the realization of my lifelong dream within reach.

As the engine roared to life and the plane taxied down the runway, my heart raced with anticipation. And then, with a gentle lift, we were airborne, soaring into the boundless expanse of the sky. The sensation of flight, of freedom, was unlike anything I had ever experienced before. With each passing moment, my excitement soared to new heights, my spirit lifting with the wind beneath our wings.

After our exhilarating flight, Carter sat me down in his office and laid out the roadmap for my flight training journey. He explained the rigorous requirements, from classroom instruction to medical exams, flight training, check rides, and ultimately, obtaining my pilot's license. It was a daunting but exciting prospect, and I knew I was ready to take on the challenge.

With determination in my heart, I signed up for the Visual Flight Rules (VFR) pilot's license program, officially committing to pursuing my dream of becoming a pilot. The stage was set for the next chapter of my life to unfold amidst the clouds and endless blue skies.

In the meantime, as I eagerly awaited the start of my flight training, I enrolled in evening classes for FAR (Federal Aviation Regulations) instruction at "Bella Vista High School, Adult Education Evening Class under the guidance of the knowledgeable ground school instructor, Bob Williams.These classes would provide me with the foundational knowledge I needed to excel in my flight training endeavors ie: Navigation using Instruments etc.

But before I could take to the skies, I needed to ensure I was medically fit for the journey ahead. So, I underwent a thorough medical examination at an FAA (Federal Aviation Administration) medical facility, ensuring that I met all the necessary requirements to embark on this adventure of a lifetime.

However, truth be told, inside, I was a nervous wreck. So many questions plagued my mind.

What if I wasn't cut out for this? What if my dream of becoming a pilot was nothing more than a fleeting fantasy?

The weight of uncertainty bore down on me like a heavy burden as I grappled with the fear of the unknown. What if I couldn't handle the rigorous training required to earn my wings? What if I faltered under the pressure, unable to rise to the challenge before me?

With each passing moment, the weight of my doubts threatened to overwhelm me, casting a shadow of doubt over my aspirations. But deep down, beneath the layers of apprehension, a flicker of determination burned bright within me. I refused to let fear dictate my fate, to let uncertainty derail my dreams.

In that moment of vulnerability, I made a choice. I chose to confront my fears head-on, to embrace the challenge before me with courage and resilience. Yes, the journey ahead would be fraught with obstacles and uncertainties, but I refused to let them define me.

I took a deep breath and pushed aside my doubts and focused on the task at hand. I may not have had all the answers, but I was determined to find them, one step at a time.

With my medical certification in hand, I was ready to spread my wings and take flight into the world of aviation.

Chapter 4

"The future belongs to those who believe in the beauty of their dreams." - Eleanor Roosevelt

The future belongs to those who believe in the beauty of their dreams. These words resonate deep within me, echoing the sentiments of hope and possibility that have guided me on my journey through life.

As I reflect on my past experiences and aspirations, I am reminded of the power of belief in shaping our destinies. From the earliest moments of childhood, I dared to dream of a future filled with promise and potential. It was this unwavering belief in the beauty of my dreams that fueled my determination to pursue them with unwavering conviction.

In the face of adversity and uncertainty, I clung to my dreams like a beacon of light in the darkness, guiding me towards a brighter tomorrow. For it is in the pursuit of our dreams that we discover the true essence of our being, unlocking hidden talents and potentialities that lay dormant within us.

But belief alone is not enough; it must be accompanied by action and perseverance. I learned this lesson firsthand as I navigated the twists and turns of life's journey, facing setbacks and challenges along the way. Yet, with each obstacle encountered, I remained steadfast in my belief in the beauty of my dreams, refusing to let go of the vision that propelled me forward.

Let me take you back to that memorable day, August 24th, 1986, when my adventure into the world of flight began.

Picture this: The Karl Harder Airport, formerly known as Lincoln Airport, buzzing with the anticipation of another day of training. There I stood, facing the Cessna 150, my heart pounding with a mix of excitement and nerves.

As I stepped onto the tarmac, I couldn't help but marvel at the sleek lines of the aircraft before me. It was my ticket to the skies, my gateway to a whole new realm of possibilities. With my instructor by my side, I embarked on the preflight procedures, my hands moving with a newfound confidence born from hours of classroom instruction.

With everything in order, it was time to takeoff. The engine roared to life, filling the air with the promise of adventure. As we soared into the sky, I felt a rush of exhilaration unlike anything I had ever experienced before. For the first time, I was truly flying.

Over the course of that first lesson, my instructor guided me through the basics: straight and level flight, climbs and glides. With each maneuver, I grew more accustomed to the feel of the controls beneath my fingertips. My instructor's calm demeanor and steady guidance helped to ease my nerves, instilling in me a sense of confidence that I never knew I possessed.

But it wasn't all smooth sailing. On September 18th, 1986, I faced my first real challenge: landings. As we made our approach, my heart raced with fear of the unknown. Would I be able to bring the plane safely to the ground?

I remember vividly the struggle I faced during those early attempts at landing. Each time I approached the runway, my heart raced with anticipation, my palms sweaty with nerves. And each time, despite my best efforts, I couldn't seem to stick the landing.

But then came that pivotal moment when Carter offered me a simple yet profound piece of advice: fly 10 feet above the runway. It seemed counterintuitive at first, but I trusted in Carter's wisdom and decided to give it a try.

As I made my approach for yet another landing attempt, I focused all my attention on maintaining that precise altitude. There was no room for error, no margin for deviation. And miraculously, I managed to scrape by on my first attempt, albeit barely.

But instead of feeling defeated, I felt a glimmer of hope. I realized that I was getting closer, inching ever nearer to mastering this essential skill. So I went around for another attempt, and then another, flying 10 feet above the runway each time.

With each subsequent attempt, my confidence grew. I could feel myself getting more comfortable, more at ease with the controls. And finally, when Carter gave me the green light to try again, I went for it with everything I had.

The landing was still a bit bumpy, far from perfect, but this time, I felt something different. I felt a sense of accomplishment, of triumph, coursing through my veins. For the first time, I truly believed that I could do it.

And as I touched down on the runway, I knew that I had crossed a significant milestone in my journey as a pilot. From that moment on, it only got easier. With each subsequent landing, I refined my technique, honed my skills, until eventually, I had mastered it.

Looking back on that experience, I realize now that it was more than just a lesson in flying—it was a lesson in perseverance, in overcoming fear, and in believing in myself.

As my journey towards becoming a pilot progressed, I found myself immersed in both practical flight training and theoretical study. Evenings were dedicated to my Federal Aviation Regulations class at Bella Vista High School, where we delved into the intricacies of aviation law and procedures. Guided by the authoritative tome “FAR: Federal Aviation Regulations for Pilots” - its pages filled with the rules and regulations governing our skies - we explored topics ranging from chart interpretation to navigation techniques.

Week after week, I eagerly absorbed the wealth of knowledge imparted by our instructor, diving deep into the complexities of calculating ground speed, airspeed, and mastering the art of navigation. The class, held once a week over a period of three months, became a cornerstone of my aviation education, laying the groundwork for a comprehensive understanding of the regulatory framework that governs the aviation industry.

As I kept up with my flight training alongside Carter, things really started to pick up speed. With every lesson, I felt like I was leveling up in the pilot game. By the time I hit the 11th lesson milestone and clocked in 20 hours of flight time, I was feeling pretty good about myself.

I mean, think about it: I had nailed down important stuff like how to work those flaps, nail those takeoffs and landings, and gracefully execute go-arounds. It was like I had unlocked a whole new set of skills and maneuvers, and man, did it feel good.

Moreover, I had ventured into the realm of cross-country navigation, tackling challenges such as dead reckoning and VOR navigation with determination and precision. These practical exercises not only tested my piloting skills but also instilled in me a sense of confidence and competence, as I navigated the skies with increasing proficiency.

With each milestone reached, I grew ever closer to my goal of earning my pilot's license. And as I continued to balance the rigors of flight training with the academic demands of my FAR class, I knew that every lesson learned and every regulation mastered brought me one step closer to realizing my dream of taking to the skies as a licensed pilot.

Chapter 5

I'm going to dedicate this chapter to Carter and my family.

I have always said having a good flight instructor is like having a seasoned guide leading you through a treacherous jungle. They're not just there to teach you how to fly; they're there to show you how to navigate the skies safely and confidently. From the moment I stepped into the cockpit with my instructor, Carter, I knew I was in good hands.

He wasn't just an instructor; he was a mentor, a coach, and a friend all rolled into one. He had a wealth of experience under his belt, and he wasn't afraid to share it. Every lesson with Carter was an adventure, filled with practical tips, theoretical knowledge, and invaluable insights gleaned from years of flying.

But what set Carter apart wasn't just his expertise; it was his passion for teaching. He genuinely cared about his students' success, and he wasn't afraid to push us out of our comfort zones to help us reach our full potential. Whether we were practicing emergency procedures or mastering complex maneuvers, Carter was there every step of the way.

And perhaps most importantly, Carter understood the importance of instilling confidence in his students. Flying can be daunting, especially for beginners, but with Carter by my side, I felt like I could take on the world. He taught me not just how to fly a plane, but how to trust in myself and my abilities, even in the face of adversity.

He didn't believe in shortcuts or easy rides. Every lesson was a challenge, designed to push his students to their limits and beyond. And I was no exception. I wasn't content with just the bare minimum. I wanted to soak up every ounce of knowledge he had to offer. From theoretical concepts to practical skills, I craved it all.

In Carter's eyes, being a pilot wasn't just about flying a plane; it was about being prepared for anything, even the most unexpected situations. And with his guidance, I was determined to become the best pilot I could possibly be.

This experience taught me that perseverance pays off. It taught me the importance of pushing past my comfort zone and embracing challenges head-on. These are lessons that I carry with me every day, whether I'm facing a difficult decision at work or navigating the ups and downs of family life.

Just as I trusted Carter to guide me through the skies, I've learned to trust in myself and my abilities. I've learned to approach life's obstacles with the same focus and determination that I brought to my flight training. And just like landing a plane, I've discovered that with patience and practice, even the most daunting challenges can be overcome.

I still remember how I felt after completing my first solo flight. It was like reaching the pinnacle of my dreams. The moment I touched down safely, I felt an overwhelming sense of accomplishment and joy that I can only describe as heavenly. It was as if I had earned my pilot's license right then and there.

I vividly remember turning to Carter with a grin from ear to ear, exclaiming that I was ready to fly around the world. My confidence soared to new heights, and I felt invincible in that moment. The skies seemed to open up before me, beckoning me to explore every corner of the globe. And oh, how perfect that landing felt! Smooth as silk, without a single bump or hitch. It was a moment of pure triumph, solidifying the realization of my dream and leaving me with an indescribable sense of fulfillment.

As I stepped out of the plane, my heart brimming with excitement, I couldn't wait to share the news with my family and friends. Their support and encouragement had been a driving force behind my journey, and I knew they would share in my elation.

Seeing the joy and pride in the faces of my wife and kids was the icing on the cake. Their happiness and pride in my achievement meant more to me than words can express. In their eyes, I could see the admiration and love they held for me, filling me with a deep sense of fulfillment and gratitude.

So many parents want their kids to follow in their footseps but one thing I'm proud of is that my wife and I have never forced our kids to pursue *our* dreams. As long as they were happy and living comfortably, we did what we could to support them. We worked tirelessly, running our own businesses – me as a Chevron dealership owner and later at the State Franchise Tax Board, and my wife at the State Department of Motor Vehicles – to ensure that our sons had the opportunities to succeed.

And it fills me with immense pride to see how far my sons, Michael and Rocky, have come in their respective careers. They've truly soared to great heights, and their success is a testament to their hard work and dedication.

Seeing them now, in positions of influence and leadership, is incredibly rewarding. It's a testament to their determination and resilience, as well as the values we instilled in them growing up. And while their paths may have been different, but both Michael and Rocky have made us proud. We've all been living our dreams and my sons are just as supportive of the path I have chosen.

Over the years, a lot of people have asked me how I felt during my first solo flight and why I still chose to become a pilot, despite having a career and family life. They couldn't fathom why I would chase after my dreams in my early thirties, when I had a family to take care of.

Let me tell you something. The first time you take off is an experience that is surreal. I can't even put it into mere words. When I sat in the cockpit, I had to mentally slap myself because I still couldn't believe it.

It wasn't just about the achievement itself; it was about the realization that I was living out a dream that had ignited within me at the tender age of five.

Tears welled up in my eyes as the weight of this realization hit me. To finally be sitting in the cockpit, to feel the hum of the engine beneath me, and to soar through the skies with nothing but the wind as my guide – it was a moment of pure, unadulterated joy. It was as if every ounce of effort, every hurdle overcome, had led me to this accomplishment. But of course, that doesn't mean there weren't any instances when panic didn't kick in, or I had to trust my gut more than my brain.

I remember when we flew to Buttes, an isolated island of mountain peaks in the valley. The adrenaline surged through my veins as Carter simulated an engine failure while we circled above the skies. With the engine off and just 2000 feet above the rugged terrain, the gravity of the situation hit me like a ton of bricks. There was no room for hesitation, no time for doubt.

Surveying the landscape below, I quickly realized that our options were limited. Gliding to safety seemed improbable, and panic threatened to take hold. But in that moment, I drew upon the emergency maneuvers I had learned, channeling every ounce of focus and determination.

With a steely resolve, I identified the best possible spot to attempt a landing amidst the towering peaks. The odds of survival were slim, but I knew that indecision was not an option. I relayed my plan to Carter, my voice steady despite the surge of adrenaline coursing through me.

As I prepared to execute the daring maneuver, Carter's calm presence beside me served as a silent reassurance. With a nod of affirmation, I committed to the course of action, fully aware of the risks involved. With Carter's guidance, the engine roared back to life just as we began our descent, narrowly avoiding disaster.

In the aftermath of the harrowing experience, Carter's words echoed in my mind – "You are one daredevil pilot if I ever saw one."

I told him it was because of him; seeing how confident he was made me forget about my worries. This is what I always tell my sons: be confident in your decisions and the answer will come to you. As cliched as it sounds, we need to believe in ourselves. We need to believe that we can overcome any obstacle in our way. And trust me, once you build up that confidence, you'll build up the courage to take on anything!

Another memory I have that I still think about is when I tried the spin maneuver/spiral maneuver.

The spiral maneuver taught me a valuable lesson about flying—it's a bit like controlling a remote-control car. Just as the car responds to the commands of its controller, an aircraft follows the directions of its pilot. But there's more to it than just pressing buttons or pulling levers.

Flying demands belief, passion, and a unique set of skills, whether they're inherent or learned. It's like guiding that remote control car with finesse and precision, but on a much grander scale. Every movement, every adjustment, is a delicate dance between the pilot and the plane.

If there's one thing I've learned from my early days of flying, it's that navigating an uncontrolled airport requires sharp focus and quick thinking. I remember a moment when I was preparing to take off, only to spot another plane coming in for a landing directly towards me. In a split second, I had to react, veering off course to avoid a potential disaster. It was a reminder of the vigilance required in the skies.

And then there are the challenges posed by mountainous terrain. When you're surrounded by peaks on either side of the runway, there's no room for error. You can't rely on gliding and landing gracefully – instead, you have to rely on your aircraft's flaps to safely navigate the descent. It's a test of skill and precision, requiring a steady hand and a keen understanding of your surroundings.

One piece of advice I have for beginners is: never panic! That's the golden rule of flying, especially in moments of uncertainty or unexpected challenges. Drawing on the knowledge and experience gained during flight training is essential, but it's also about applying a healthy dose of common sense and staying calm under pressure.

Keeping a watchful eye on your surroundings is key, anticipating potential hazards and preparing to respond swiftly and decisively. It's about being ready to execute maneuvers and decisions that you might never have imagined needing to make, but which become essential in the face of unforeseen circumstances.

In the cockpit, staying level-headed and focused can mean the difference between a smooth flight and a potentially dangerous situation. So, remember to trust in your training, rely on your instincts, and always keep a cool head, no matter what challenges may arise.

Chapter 6

October 19th, 1986 was a day that started like any other at the airport. Preflight checks, gearing up for another session with Carter, my trusty flight instructor. Little did I know, this day would mark a significant milestone in my journey to becoming a pilot.

Carter and I went through the usual routine, but there was a twist in store. After two takeoffs and landings under his watchful eye, he dropped a bombshell: *I was going solo for the next round!*

I must admit, I was taken aback but not entirely surprised. With Carter's rigorous training (regiment), I knew I was ready for this moment. So, with a mix of nerves and excitement, I taxied the plane onto the taxiway "and prepared to take off."

As I revved up the engine and announced my intentions over the radio, a surge of adrenaline kicked in. Full throttle, and I was off, climbing into the sky with a newfound sense of freedom. The patterns felt familiar, almost like second nature, and before I knew it, I was making a smooth touchdown on the runway.

Relief washed over me as I realized I'd aced my first solo takeoff and landing. But what struck me most was the absence of fear. Carter's unwavering confidence in my abilities had rubbed off on me, turning what could have been a nerve-wracking experience into a moment of triumph.

With a hearty pat on the back from Carter and his words of praise ringing in my ears, I knew I was one step closer to my dream of becoming a pilot. And so, with a newfound spring in my step, I looked forward to the next chapter in my aviation adventure.

Navigating crosswinds during takeoffs and landings is like dancing with Mother Nature herself—challenging yet exhilarating. My flight instructor drilled into me the importance of mastering these maneuvers, especially in unpredictable weather conditions. After all, there's no room for error when it comes to the delicate balance of lift and gravity.

The key lesson? Never aim for perfection, especially when faced with crosswinds or turbulent winds. Trying to "grease the wheels" might sound enticing, but it's a recipe for disaster. Instead, it's all about maintaining control and making calculated adjustments based on instinct, experience, and a touch of gut feeling.

Imagine you're on the final approach, the wind tugging at your wings, and every fiber of your being screaming for precision. But here's the kicker—crosswind corrections start way before you even hit that final stretch. It's a delicate dance of anticipation, where instincts and calculations collide to keep you safely on course.

And let me tell you, no two crosswind scenarios are alike. Each runway presents its own unique challenge, demanding a keen eye and a steady hand. But with experience comes wisdom, and soon enough, you'll find yourself making split-second adjustments with the finesse of a seasoned pro.

In fact, I was so well-prepared for the challenge that I took my check ride on a blustery day and aced it with flying colors. It was a testament to the rigorous training and unwavering dedication instilled in me by my instructor.

The journey was far from over. With half of my classroom training under my belt, I was ready to tackle the next level of challenges head-on. As they say, when the going gets tough, the tough get going.

On one crisp October day, the complexity of our flight maneuvers escalated. We delved into the intricacies of short field takeoffs and landings, where precision was paramount and every inch of the runway counted. The adrenaline rush of mastering these maneuvers was electrifying, pushing me to new heights of skill and confidence.

But the real thrill came the following day—October 26th, 1986—a date etched into my memory as the day I faced the ultimate test of courage and skill: the spiral/spin experience. Carter, ever the daredevil, proposed this exhilarating challenge. With a mix of excitement and trepidation, I asked him to elaborate.

His explanation was simple yet thrilling. We would ascend to a dizzying 8500 feet altitude, only to plummet straight down with a flick of the rudder; either to the right or the left. It was a gravity-defying adventure unlike any other, promising to test my mettle in the most exhilarating way possible.

On November 1st, 1986, I had a big day in my flight training. Each lesson was getting tougher, but I was ready for the challenge. This time, we focused on flying from one place to another, which is super important for pilots. We started at Lincoln Airport, then went to Woodland Airport, then Sacramento Executive Airport, and finally back to Lincoln.

After that, things got even more intense. We flew to different airports in the foothills—places like Cameron Park, Georgetown, Placerville, and Auburn. Landing there was tricky because of the winds swirling around the mountains. It was like a real-life video game, dodging obstacles and making split-second decisions.

Our journey led us to Cameron Park Airport, a place filled with memories from my past. Back in the summer of 1968, I worked at Cameron Park Country Club as a greenskeeper under my relative, Raj, who was the Golf Course Superintendent. Those were simpler times, and Cameron Park was still in its early stages of development.

At that time, the airport was a humble spot with just one airplane and a solitary house near the runway's end. Both belonged to the owner and developer of the Cameron Park properties. The airplane, a Cessna 172 fixed-wing, caught my eye every time I passed by. I'd take breaks from my duties to wander over, admiring its sleek design and imagining myself flying it one day.

As I drove around on my trusty Cushman scooter, marking missing stakes from the lots, the allure of aviation grew stronger. Little did I know that years later, I'd return to this very airport to fulfill my childhood dream of taking flight. It felt like fate had brought me back to where it all began, a full-circle moment that filled me with gratitude and excitement.

The moment before taking off from Lincoln Airport to Cameron Park Airport was simply awe-inspiring. As I prepared for landing at Cameron Park, my mind struggled to grasp the reality of what I was about to achieve. The sheer joy and fulfillment I felt were overwhelming, to say the least.

Anyway, after touchdown, an indescribable sense of satisfaction washed over me. Tears threatened to spill from my eyes as I stood beside my plane, filled with gratitude and disbelief. Landing at Cameron Park Airport surpassed anything I had ever imagined, turning a once-distant fantasy into a tangible reality. It was a moment of pure bliss and fulfillment, etched into my memory forever.

Then I learned a valuable lesson: **Never apply or release the flaps abruptly!**

Next was Georgetown Airport which was just a short 15-minute flight away, and we touched down smoothly without encountering any issues. It's worth noting that all these foothills' airports were uncontrolled, meaning pilots had to rely on airport radio frequencies to coordinate takeoffs and landings.

Next up was Placerville Airport, nestled atop the highest mountain in the area. This unique location gives it a tabletop appearance, almost like landing in the sky. Because of its elevation and layout, there was no need to use flaps for takeoff or landing. I simply glided in, executed a touch-and-go maneuver, and was airborne again in no time.

Surrounded by clear skies and no towering peaks or structures in sight, it was a serene descent from our cruising altitude of 5000 feet to the airport's mountainous perch at around 2000 feet above sea level. With no obstacles to navigate, the landing was as smooth as gliding on a gentle breeze. Similarly, taking off required no flaps; the runway's elevation and clear surroundings made for a straightforward departure.

While flaps weren't necessary for this particular takeoff and landing, they're often employed for their ability to facilitate a swift climb. Some airports mandate short field takeoffs to minimize noise disturbance to nearby communities, but thankfully, we didn't encounter such restrictions during our flight—things were simpler in the Stone Age (*Just kidding!)*

Navigating through mountainous terrain presents its own set of challenges, especially when you encounter air pockets and turbulent conditions. The thermal air currents can toss you around, potentially veering you off course if you're not vigilant. Despite the bumps along the way, maintaining an accurate compass heading is crucial to ensure you stay on track and reach your intended airports safely.

Our journey continued to Auburn Airport, where we encountered no difficulties during landing. It's important to mention that pilots always take off and land against the wind, using orange or red wind socks to determine wind direction.

As we prepared to depart for Lincoln Airport, I had a close call when I noticed another plane approaching to land in my direction. Swift action and clear communication averted disaster, highlighting the importance of vigilance in the skies. With the situation resolved, I took off for the final leg of our journey and safely touched down at Lincoln Airport.

The following day, our focus shifted to mastering emergency maneuvers and honing our radio communication skills. Our training route took us from Lincoln Airport to Marysville Airport, then onward to Oroville Airport before circling back to our starting point.

Our journey began smoothly, with a safe landing at Marysville Airport followed by a seamless departure to Oroville Airport. After touching down at Oroville, we took a brief respite, indulging in a well-deserved sandwich while discussing our next leg of the journey. Carter outlined our plan to fly to Truckee Airport, prompting me to meticulously chart our course, calculating distances, ground speeds, air speeds, headings, estimated arrival times, and identifying prominent landmarks along the way.

As I prepared for takeoff in the trusty Cessna 150, I followed protocol, announcing our departure on the airport frequency radio. Little did I know, an unexpected obstacle awaited us at Truckee Airport: a deceased cow obstructing the runway. With quick thinking, Carter and I discussed our options. Auburn Airport was snowed in, leaving Lincoln Airport as our only viable alternative.

With confidence, I assured Carter that we'd touch down at precisely 1:01pm. He questioned my certainty, but I was resolute in my calculations, ready to prove myself. As we descended for landing, a sudden twist: an engine failure simulation. Without hesitation, I went through the emergency checklist, checking fuel levels and initiating a glide towards Lincoln Airport.

Maintaining focus amidst the adrenaline rush, I carefully monitored the wind direction, ensuring a safe approach. Carter praised me for my performance and he gave me a pat on the back for exceeding his expectations.

The following day, brimming with confidence, I tackled another cross-country flight to Marysville Airport and back. With 35 hours of flight training under my belt and graduation from Bella Vista High School's classroom instruction, I was primed for success. A stellar score of 95% on the FAA written test only fueled my excitement for the next milestone: the check ride.

On November 22, 1986, my instructor announced my certification to fly the Cessna 172. After completing preflight checks, we soared to remote areas of the airport, practicing steep turns, stalls, and solo takeoffs and landings. Carter's approval paved the way for my longest solo cross-country flight yet, where I'd put my newfound skills to the test. With thorough flight planning, weather checks, and communication protocols in place, I was ready to conquer the skies.

The basic instruments training I received was crucial and had saved my life.

The unpredictability of the weather, from haze and fog to heavy downpours and sandstorms, can pose significant challenges, even for seasoned pilots. It was a skill set that proved invaluable during my 300-mile cross country flight.

When unexpectedly caught in a dense fog, my training kicked in, and I relied on my knowledge and experience to navigate safely. Utilizing the Air Radar Service Area (ARSA), I was guided out of the hazardous conditions and back on track. Understanding how to interpret instruments and their functions became second nature, ultimately saving my life in a moment of crisis.

Chapter 7

With the dawn of November 23, 1986, excitement bubbled within me as I prepared for my longest cross-country flight yet. The itinerary was set: from Lincoln Airport to Fresno Airport, then onward to Napa Airport, before circling back to my starting point. Every detail was meticulously attended to during preflight checks, from scrutinizing the aircraft's condition to confirming the weather forecast with the airport authorities. With my flight plan filed and clearance granted, I embarked on this exhilarating journey.

The day greeted me with crystal-clear skies, a promising backdrop for adventure. As I fired up the engine of my trusty Cessna 172, anticipation coursed through my veins. With a gentle push of the throttle, I soared into the boundless expanse above.

Navigating the airspace, I reached out to Oakland Air Radar Service Area for guidance, their voices crackling through the headset amidst the hum of the engine. Transitioning over Modesto, I seamlessly switched frequencies to Castle Air Force Base ARSA, their directives guiding me ever closer to my first destination: Fresno.

Approaching Fresno Airport, I established contact with the control tower, their reassuring instructions guiding me through the final stages of descent. With practiced precision, I executed the landing, the runway stretching out before me like a welcoming embrace.

As the wheels kissed the tarmac, a sense of accomplishment washed over me. But there was little time to bask in the moment, for my journey was far from over.

Soon, I embarked on my journey to Napa Airport, the skies initially seemed cooperative, with my aircraft cruising steadily at 6500 feet. However, as I progressed, ominous patches of haze began to obscure the landscape below. Instinctively, I reached out to Castle Air Force Base (ARSA) for guidance, but my calls echoed unanswered through the ether. With each passing moment, the haze thickened, morphing into an impenetrable fog that engulfed my aircraft.

Faced with this unexpected challenge, I recalled the advice of my flight instructor, Carter, whose unwavering confidence had become my beacon of strength. Remembering his words – "The only thing we fear is fear itself."

I steeled myself for the ordeal ahead. With a newfound resolve, I initiated emergency protocols, beginning a gradual descent to 1500 feet while scanning the terrain below for a suitable landing spot.

Amidst the dense fog, a narrow winding road snaked through the canyon, but its treacherous twists offered little hope for a safe touchdown. Then, like a beacon of hope amidst the gloom, a patch of dense forest emerged, its dense canopy promising a cushioned impact. With determination coursing through my veins, I set my sights on this makeshift runway, ready to face whatever fate awaited me.

As I prepared for my final descent, a sense of calm washed over me, my mind focused on executing the emergency landing with precision. Just as I braced myself to transmit a distress call, the crackle of the radio pierced the silence, Castle AFB (ARSA) breaking through the static with an apologetic explanation – they had been on an unexpected coffee break.

Relief flooded my senses as their reassuring voices guided me through the fog, orchestrating my ascent to safer altitudes and providing me with the compass heading needed to navigate out of the perilous shroud. With their unwavering support, I emerged from the fog's clutches, emerging into the welcoming embrace of clear skies beyond Modesto Airport.

Expressing my heartfelt gratitude, I bid farewell to Castle AFB (ARSA), their voices fading as I reached out to Oakland (ARSA) to continue my journey. With renewed determination, I pressed onward, following the familiar landmarks that dotted my flight plan, until finally, the sight of Napa Airport beckoned in the distance.

Guided by the steady voice of Napa Control Tower, I executed a flawless landing, my spirit soaring with the realization that I had conquered the unforeseen challenges that had threatened to derail my journey. After a brief respite to refuel both my aircraft and my spirits, I was once again ready to take to the skies.

Now, prepare for something even more interesting...

As I geared up for my flight back to Lincoln Airport from Napa, everything seemed set for a smooth takeoff. But just as I was about to hit the runway, my heart dropped – the fuel gauge showed empty! It was a rookie mistake, and I felt a wave of panic.

Quickly radioing the control tower, I explained my situation as a student pilot and the urgent need for fuel. They calmly directed me back to the terminal, where the fueling station awaited. Racing against time, I taxied to the fueling area, hoping for a quick fix.

There, I faced a moment of irony – I owned a Chevron Station, yet I'd forgotten the golden rule: always top up the tank. Despite this slip-up, the attendants assured me that a mere 8 gallons would do the trick. It was a wake-up call – in aviation, you can never be too prepared.

Lesson learned, I vowed never to underestimate the importance of being ready for anything in the skies!

With the tank topped up, I felt a renewed sense of confidence as I taxied back to the runway threshold. Before proceeding, I radioed the ground control crew to inform them of my refueling and readiness to take off. With their clearance, I eagerly lined up for takeoff, the anticipation building with each passing moment.

As I soared into the sky, I relied on my VOR navigation to guide me towards Sacramento. Along the way, I couldn't help but marvel at the sight of Travis Air Force Base below me, where a massive C-5 aircraft was taking off, dwarfing everything in its vicinity. Despite the close proximity to military airspace, I maintained my compliance altitude and promptly alerted Oakland ARSA of the situation.

Upon reaching Sacramento Executive Airport, I bid farewell to Oakland ARSA and turned to my trusty chart to navigate the final leg of my journey back to Lincoln Airport. Excitement bubbled within me as I envisioned completing three celebratory touch-and-go maneuvers upon my return.

As I approached Lincoln Airport, the thrill of accomplishment coursed through my veins. But just as I touched down on the runway, my heart skipped a beat as the engine suddenly sputtered and died. Shocked and bewildered, I scanned the horizon for assistance and spotted the Fuel Tank Mobile Truck nearby. With a quick call for help, the driver rushed to my aid, assisting me in safely pushing my plane off the runway.

It was then that the truth dawned on me – I had run out of fuel once again. The meager 8 gallons provided by the gas station attendant at Napa Airport had only been enough to get me this far. I learned *another* valuable lesson—don't trust anyone to refuel your tank!

After safely parking my plane, I made my way to the airport facility to find my flight instructor, Carter. Excitedly, I recounted the entire adventure of my longest cross-country flight, detailing every twist and turn of my solo journey. Carter listened intently, his expression a mix of astonishment and relief as he absorbed the gravity of the situation.

Making it through the unexpected challenges of my flight showed just how important Mr. Carter's training and confidence were. He taught me the skills and determination I needed to handle whatever came my way in the sky.

Chapter 8

November 29, 1986, a crisp evening setting the stage for a thrilling adventure into the night skies. It was the kickoff of my night flight training, and my instructor had one instruction: bring the brightest flashlight I could find. Little did I know, it was the beginning of an exhilarating journey under the stars.

Some of you might be wondering why I was told to bring a flashlight as it doesn't really make sense for us to. In my mind, I envisioned using the flashlight to beam light onto the runway during our nighttime takeoffs and landings. So, I made sure to bring the biggest, brightest flashlight I could find, thinking it would come in handy for lighting up the darkness below.

Little did I know, Carter had a different plan in mind. As we prepared for our night flight and he explained the purpose of the flashlight, I realized its true importance. It wasn't for the runway at all—it was to illuminate the instruments inside the cockpit once the lights were turned off, allowing us to navigate through the pitch darkness of the sky.

As I prepared for the night ahead, I couldn't help but feel a tinge of excitement mixed with a hint of apprehension. With my trusty flashlight in hand, I embarked on the preflight checks, ensuring every detail was in place for the upcoming challenge.

A lot of people ask if the preflight procedure is the same as the day flying one. Before embarking on our night flight, the preflight procedure mirrored that of our daytime flights. We meticulously checked every aspect of the aircraft to ensure its safety and readiness for the journey ahead.

First and foremost, we inspected the gas tank to ensure there was no water at the bottom, a precaution essential for smooth and uninterrupted flight. We also examined the fuselage closely, scanning for any signs of damage or loose rivets that could compromise our safety in the air.

Of course, we couldn't overlook the condition of the wheels, ensuring they were fully intact and free from any flats that could hinder our landing. Additionally, we double-checked the functionality of crucial lights, including the landing lights and beacon light, essential for visibility in the dark.

Anyway, with the runway lights illuminating the path ahead, my instructor Carter and I soared into the darkness, our plane cutting through the night with precision. The first round in the pattern felt like a familiar dance, but then came the real test: lights out.

With the landing lights extinguished and the runway cloaked in darkness, I relied solely on instinct and skill as we navigated the inky blackness.

Navigating through pitch darkness during the night flight was an experience like no other. Without the comforting glow of the moon or the reassuring lights of the city below, the darkness enveloped us entirely. It was as if we were floating in a void, with only the occasional twinkle of stars above.

Finding the runway amidst this darkness was akin to searching for a needle in a haystack. From above, it appeared as a faint, narrow strip, barely distinguishable from the surrounding terrain. Yet, despite the daunting challenge, we had to adhere to the standard takeoff and landing procedures, all while ensuring we stayed on course and avoided any potential mishaps.

But thanks to Carter's exceptional teaching, navigating through this darkness became more manageable with each passing moment. His guidance was like a steady beacon, illuminating the path ahead and instilling in me the confidence to tackle even the most daunting of challenges. With every lesson, it felt as though another layer of uncertainty was peeled away, revealing the clarity and certainty that lay beneath.

But we didn't stop there. With the runway lights switched off entirely, I faced the ultimate test of my night flying prowess. With nerves of steel, I took to the skies, using nothing but my wits and the remote control to guide us safely back to earth. It was a triumphant moment as I proved to myself and my instructor that I was more than capable of handling the night sky.

As we wrapped up our training, Carter surprised me by stepping out of the plane, leaving me to navigate the night alone. With confidence coursing through my veins, I took control.

But before embarking on my solo flight from Lincoln Airport, we made a pit stop at Sacramento Executive Airport, which boasted a control tower. There, I needed to complete 10 touch-and-go landings to fulfill the necessary requirements. With each landing, the process seemed to flow more smoothly, and the maneuvers became increasingly second nature.

Following that, I dedicated three hours to night flight training, covering all the essential requirements. As the hours passed and the training progressed, the challenges of navigating through the darkness gradually became more manageable. With each successful maneuver, I gained confidence and proficiency, until finally, I completed all the necessary night flying requirements.

As I reflected on the culmination of my night flight training, I couldn't help but feel a sense of accomplishment and gratitude. The challenges I faced, from navigating through pitch darkness to mastering precise landings, had tested my skills and pushed me beyond my comfort zone. Yet, with the guidance of my instructor and the resilience I discovered within myself, I had overcome each obstacle.

As I looked ahead to the next phase of my aviation journey, I carried with me the lessons learned during those nights in the sky. The importance of preparation, the value of unwavering confidence, and the thrill of conquering new heights were all etched into my being.

With a renewed sense of purpose and a deep-seated passion for flight, I was eager to continue my pursuit of a private pilot's license. The night flight training had been a transformative experience, solidifying my commitment to aviation and setting the stage for the adventures yet to come.

Chapter 9

On February 14, 1987, my flight instructor, Carter Flygare, officially certified me as having completed all the necessary training and requirements for the Private Pilot Rating under FAA regulations. With his signature, I was given the green light for the check ride, a crucial step toward obtaining my pilot's license. Eager to move forward, I promptly scheduled the check ride for February 18th, 1987, and informed Carter of my plans.

However, on the morning of February 18th, Carter called me with news that the weather conditions were unfavorable for the check ride. Strong north winds were blowing at over 23 knots per hour, making it less than ideal for flying. Despite the warning, I felt confident in my abilities to handle challenging weather conditions and decided to proceed with the check ride as scheduled.

I had been waiting for this moment for so long, dreaming of flying high above the clouds. Even if the weather wasn't great, nothing could stop me from chasing my dreams.

Upon arriving at Lincoln Airport, I met with Lt. Col. Karl Harder from the FAA, who would be administering the check ride. Despite the windy conditions, I was determined to demonstrate my proficiency. Karl verified my logbook and tested me on pre-check ride procedures, which I successfully completed. Despite Karl's hesitation due to the weather, I expressed my conviction that I was prepared to undertake the test.

As we began the check ride, Karl tested me on various maneuvers and procedures. Despite the challenging conditions, I executed each task to the best of my ability. The check ride lasted 1.4 hours, during which I remained focused and composed. Upon landing safely back at Lincoln Airport, Karl remained silent, leaving me uncertain of my performance.

The uncertainty gnawed at me, and Karl's vague responses only added to my anxiety. I was torn between the fear of failure and the belief that I had performed admirably.

With no immediate feedback from Karl, I left the airport, awaiting news of my results. Despite my confidence in my performance, the uncertainty lingered throughout the day as I eagerly awaited Karl's decision.

At 7:00 pm, Karl Harder called me and invited me to his home. With his address in hand, I headed over. When I arrived, he greeted me warmly and ushered me inside. Taking a seat at his conference table, he offered me a drink. I opted for water, but Karl insisted on something a bit more celebratory—vodka and orange juice. Reluctantly, I agreed.

As Karl poured our drinks, his wife Betty joined us and began typing up my certificate. Despite the festive atmosphere, I still didn't know whether I had passed the check ride. Then, to my surprise, Karl raised his glass and toasted, "Congratulations to our newest pilot, Mahendra Jagir!" It was official – I had passed!

Overwhelmed with excitement, I downed my drink in one gulp. Karl handed me my temporary pilot's license and shook my hand, commending me for my daring spirit and reminding me to always fly safely.

It felt like a dream, utterly surreal. The realization that I had become a pilot was almost too much to grasp. This was the culmination of a lifelong dream, something I had yearned for since I was a child. Yet, even as I sit here now, reflecting on it, a part of me still struggles to believe that I've actually achieved it.

It was a moment of great pride and honor to receive my Private Pilot's License with Karl Harder's signature on it, knowing his esteemed history as a pilot for General McArthur during the Korean War. Though he passed away in 1995, his legacy lives on.

Grateful for Karl and Betty Lou's hospitality and for their part in my achievement, I returned home to share the news with my family. With hugs and kisses, I told my sons, Michael and Rocky, that I was now a pilot and promised to take them flying someday.

A lot of people still ask me how I managed everything. I know it sounds easy and I probably made it seem that way, but trust me, it wasn't.

I dedicated myself to my business, working tirelessly for 16 hours a day. To ensure I could pursue my passion for flying, I hired a helper to assist during slower periods, allowing me a few precious hours to take to the skies. Despite my busy schedule, I made sure to be present during peak and early morning hours to manage daily operations, handle bookkeeping, and make bank deposits. Balancing all aspects of my business, I still found time to pursue flight instruction, attending night classes to complete my flight ground school. Though it was challenging, I was fortunate to have exceptional teachers who guided me every step of the way.

Chapter 10

The day after receiving my pilot's license, I eagerly decided to embark on a joy ride. Excitement coursed through me as I meticulously conducted my preflight inspection. Checking every detail, I ensured the aircraft was in top condition—fuselage intact, tires properly inflated, and fuel free of water. Although I couldn't physically reach the gas cap to confirm its tightness, I trusted the fueling service attendant who had fueled the aircraft. Satisfied with the visual and technical inspections, I prepared for my maiden flight as a licensed pilot.

With anticipation bubbling within me, I transmitted my announcement over the airport frequency radio, signaling my readiness for takeoff. As I throttled down the runway, my excitement was abruptly interrupted by a deafening rattling noise emanating from the plane. Panic surged through me; I feared the worst—a catastrophic engine failure. Trapped in mid-air with insufficient runway to land, I grappled with a sense of impending doom.

Amidst the chaos, I clung to my determination, refusing to succumb to panic. Focused on completing my mission, I persevered through the unsettling noise, determined to land safely. With each circuit around the pattern, the rattling intensified, amplifying my anxiety. Yet, driven by sheer willpower, I guided the aircraft to a smooth landing.

Relieved but shaken, I taxied to my hangar and cut the ignition, eager to identify the source of the unsettling noise. To my astonishment, I discovered the gas cap dangling from the wing, its chain tethering it to the fuel tank. Though relieved by the harmless explanation, I couldn't shake off my sense of dismay. I promptly reported the incident to Carter, who, though displeased, assured me he would address the issue promptly.

Next Day, The Flight with My Son, Michael

On that sunny May morning in 1987, the anticipation of sharing my love for flying with my son, Michael, filled me with excitement. As we arrived at Lincoln Airport, the thrill of embarking on our first flight together as father and son was palpable. With the aircraft fueled up and the preflight checks completed, we eagerly boarded the plane, ready for adventure.

As we taxied down the runway and lifted off into the clear blue sky, Michael's eyes widened with wonder and excitement. From his seat beside me, he gazed out the window in awe as the landscape below us slowly transformed into a tapestry of patchwork fields and winding rivers.

Flying towards Marysville Airport, I pointed out landmarks and explained the basics of flying to Michael, who listened intently, his curiosity piqued by every detail. Despite his young age, he displayed a remarkable eagerness to learn and experience the thrill of flight firsthand.

As we approached Marysville Airport for our first landing, I guided the plane smoothly towards the runway, preparing for the descent. However, as the wheels touched down, the aircraft bounced slightly, causing a momentary jolt that caught us both by surprise. Michael let out a gasp, and I couldn't help but chuckle nervously at the unexpected bumpiness of the landing.

Upon landing, we taxied to a stop, and Michael eagerly unbuckled his seatbelt, his face beaming with excitement. Together, we inspected the aircraft, checking for any signs of damage from the landing. Despite Michael's initial concern about the scrape on the tail end of the plane, we were relieved to find that it was merely a superficial mark, with no significant harm done to the aircraft.

After ensuring that the plane was in good condition, we shared a moment of laughter and relief, marveling at the unexpected twist in our adventure. With spirits lifted and a newfound sense of camaraderie, we embarked on the return journey to Lincoln Airport, cherishing every moment of our father-son bonding experience in the skies.

Upon landing back at Lincoln Airport, we were greeted by the familiar sight of the runway and the bustling activity of the airport. As we disembarked from the plane, Michael turned to me with a wide grin, his eyes shining with excitement and pride. “That was amazing, Dad!” he exclaimed, his enthusiasm infectious.

To celebrate our successful flight, we decided to indulge in a special treat—a Hamburger Party at McDonald’s. Sitting together at a table adorned with colorful balloons and streamers, we savored the taste of victory and the joy of accomplishment. As we laughed, joked, and shared stories of our adventure, I couldn’t help but feel a deep sense of gratitude for the opportunity to share such a memorable experience with my son.

In that moment, surrounded by the simple pleasures of good food and great company, I realized that becoming a private pilot wasn't just about fulfilling a lifelong dream—it was about creating lasting memories and forging bonds that would last a lifetime. And as we raised our hamburgers in a toast to our shared adventure, I knew that this was just the beginning of many more flights to come, each one filled with new adventures and unforgettable moments shared between father and son.

But then…the Chevron's Ground Lease Expired!

In 1989, the lease for my Chevron Station came to its inevitable end, leaving me facing the painful task of packing up and closing down. Every moment of that final day felt like a dagger to my heart, filled with a profound sense of loss and sorrow.

As I gathered my personal belongings, each item seemed to carry with it memories of better days, days when the station buzzed with activity and life. Now, it stood empty and silent, a stark reminder of the passage of time and the inevitability of change.

The hardest part came when I had to let go of my employees. These people had stood by my side through thick and thin, and now I had to tell them that their jobs were gone. The look of shock and disappointment on their faces was a crushing blow, one that weighed heavily on my conscience.

Walking through the deserted aisles of the Chevron Station, I couldn't shake the feeling of emptiness that filled the air. Every corner seemed to echo with the laughter and chatter of customers long gone, leaving behind only a hollow silence.

Locking up the station for the last time felt like closing the door on a chapter of my life that I had never expected to end. It was a moment of profound sadness, a final farewell to a place that had been so much more than just a business to me.

But even as I turned the key and walked away, I knew that this was not the end. It was merely the beginning of a new chapter, one filled with uncertainty and challenges, but also with the hope of new opportunities and fresh starts.

After this, I decided that I needed to take a much-needed vacation. It was the only way I would be able to have some normalcy in my life; the only way I would be able to distract my mind.

After bidding a tearful farewell to my family at the airport, especially my son Rocky, whose cries nearly broke my resolve, I embarked on a journey to Sydney, Australia, accompanied by a friend eager for adventure. The weight of leaving my loved ones behind hung heavy on my heart, but promises of bringing back souvenirs and toys for my little ones eased the ache, though only slightly.

Our journey began with a flight from Sacramento Metropolitan Airport to Los Angeles, where we awaited our connecting flight to Sydney. The anticipation of exploring a new land mingled with thoughts of home as we boarded the Qantas Airlines flight over the vast expanse of the Pacific Ocean.

Hours stretched into eternity as the endless ocean below offered no respite from the longing for familiar faces. Our brief stopover in Tahiti for refueling provided a glimpse of tropical beauty amidst the dense jungles, reminiscent of Fiji's allure. Despite the weariness of the long journey, the promise of Sydney's sights and sounds awaited us.

Arriving in Sydney, exhaustion melted away as we were warmly welcomed by friends and family, who graciously hosted us and treated us to an exhilarating tour of the city. From the iconic Sydney Opera House to the majestic Sydney Harbor Bridge, every landmark spoke of a vibrant city teeming with life and culture. Yet, amidst the excitement, a part of me yearned for my family's presence to share in the wonders I beheld.

After immersing ourselves in Sydney's charms, our journey continued to Canberra, only to encounter an unexpected obstacle at the airport. Shocked to learn of a strike affecting our intended airline, we were relieved to find an alternative in Colombian Airlines. Boarding the plane, we settled into our seats, eager to continue our adventure, albeit with a slight twist of fate.

And Now…Fasten Your Seatbelts…

As we settled into our seats on the Colombian Airlines flight to Canberra, the excitement of our journey lingered in the air. Suddenly, the cabin crew whisked in with trays of snacks and refreshments, signaling a brief respite from the anticipation of our destination.

Amidst the chatter and munching, a sharp noise pierced the air, drawing our attention to the right engine. My friend's eyes widened as he claimed to see flames shooting out from it. I chuckled, reassuring him that it was just his imagination, all in the name of keeping our fellow passenger's calm. However, deep down, I sensed something wasn't quite right.

The stewardesses hurried us along, signaling that it was time to wrap up our snacks. Hastily, we complied, but my unease grew as another explosion rattled the cabin, this time accompanied by a burst of flames from the same engine. With a quick flick, the captain shut it down, and the plane veered into a wide left turn, aiming back towards Sydney Airport.

Despite my efforts to remain composed, worry gnawed at me. Thoughts raced through my mind – who would take care of my kids if something went wrong? In that moment, I turned to prayer, seeking solace and strength.

Finally, the Sydney skyline loomed into view, and the captain's voice crackled over the intercom, announcing the need for an emergency landing. My friend's anxiety was palpable, but I reassured him that pilots were trained to handle such situations with precision and poise.

With a jolt, the plane touched down safely, and a collective sigh of relief swept through the cabin. Without missing a beat, we exchanged our tickets, redirecting our journey towards Brisbane, Australia.

Reflecting on the ordeal, I realized the importance of remaining calm and making sound decisions, even in the face of adversity. It was a lesson learned in the midst of chaos – to stay steady, never panic, and always move forward.

It's the 90s; My Youngest is Six and We're Going for a Joy Ride!

In 1990, as my younger son celebrated his sixth birthday, I remembered the promise I made to myself – to take both of my boys on a plane ride when they turned six. The moment had finally arrived.

With excitement bubbling over, I surprised them with a trip to Sacramento Executive Airport. As we approached the plane, I could see the hesitation in my youngest son's eyes. He clung to me, tears streaming down his face, adamant that none of us should fly.

Determined to fulfill my promise, I turned to my friend and flight instructor, Carter Flygare, for help. With his reassurance, my youngest son reluctantly agreed to join us in the plane.

As we soared through the skies, I watched the wonder in my sons' eyes, their fear melting away with each passing moment. The joy on their faces made every challenge worth it.

Upon landing, I couldn't help but feel a sense of accomplishment. I thanked Carter for his support and guidance, knowing that without him, this moment would not have been possible.

Together, we celebrated our successful mission at a nearby pizza place, savoring the memories of our unforgettable adventure in the sky. And as we enjoyed our meal, I couldn't help but reflect on the gratitude I felt for Carter's invaluable role in making my dream a reality.

A Better, Brighter Future

In 1998, my journey at the Franchise Tax Board (FTB) commenced as a seasonal worker, tasked with managing the influx of incoming mail. It was a humble beginning, but one filled with determination and a desire to prove myself. Despite the repetitive nature of the tasks, I approached each day with a sense of purpose, knowing that my hard work would not go unnoticed.

As the weeks passed, my dedication caught the attention of management, who recognized my commitment to excellence. Before long, I found myself receiving an unexpected promotion to the file room of the Legal Department. Stepping into this new role, I embraced the opportunity to immerse myself in the intricacies of legal documents and procedures.

The days in the file room were both challenging and rewarding. I meticulously updated files, ensuring that every piece of correspondence was accounted for and organized with precision. It was during this time that I forged connections with the attorneys who frequented the room, engaging in lively conversations and even participating in mock presentations to prepare for BOE's Appeals Court hearings.

With each passing month, I continued to prove myself as a valuable asset to the FTB. My work ethic and professionalism did not go unnoticed, leading to further opportunities for advancement. When offered the chance to pursue a legal career with the FTB's support, I humbly declined, recognizing that my passion lay elsewhere.

Instead, I found myself transitioning to a role as a Tax Technician at the call center. Here, I became the voice of guidance for taxpayers, navigating complex regulations with patience and clarity. My ability to educate and empower taxpayers earned me respect among colleagues and taxpayers alike.

As the years went by, I continued to ascend the ranks within the FTB, taking on roles of increasing responsibility and leadership. From liaising between the Governor's office and the FTB to serving as a Senior Compliance Representative, I approached each challenge with a sense of purpose and determination.

However, it was not just my professional accomplishments that defined my time at the FTB. I also found fulfillment in fostering teamwork and collaboration among colleagues. When tensions arose among team leads, I stepped into the role of Ambassador, working tirelessly to bridge divides and promote a sense of unity.

In one defining moment, I found myself leading a transformative exercise during a meeting with management and colleagues. Armed with magazines and scissors, each team created a collage reflecting their aspirations. When it was my turn to interpret our creation, I spoke passionately about the power of teamwork and the potential for greatness when we come together as one.

As my time at the FTB drew to a close in 2013, I reflected on the incredible journey I had undertaken. Though offered opportunities for further advancement, my heart led me back to my family, where I found the truest fulfillment. My legacy at the FTB was one of hard work, integrity, and a relentless commitment to excellence.

Chapter 11

"Life is a journey that you are never fully prepared for," they say. It's a winding path through valleys of joy and peaks of sorrow, a road fraught with unexpected twists and turns.

Like a ship navigating treacherous waters, we sail through storms of uncertainty and bask in the calm of moments cherished.

Each step forward is a leap of faith, each setback a lesson learned. Life's journey is akin to climbing a mountain, where every stumble teaches resilience and every climb strengthens the spirit. In the end, it's not about reaching the summit unscathed, but about the courage to continue the ascent, knowing that the view from the top is worth every struggle endured along the way.

As Robert Frost once said, "Two roads diverged in a wood, and I—I took the one less traveled by, and that has made all the difference." Indeed, it's the journey itself that shapes us, molding our hearts and souls into vessels capable of weathering life's greatest storms.

My journey to becoming a pilot was a rollercoaster of unexpected twists and turns, a tale I never could have scripted myself. As I look back on it now, I realize how improbable it all seemed at the outset. The dream of taking to the skies felt like a distant fantasy, a star shining just beyond my reach. Yet, life had other plans in store for me, weaving a narrative that defied my expectations at every turn.

There were moments when I doubted whether I would ever see that dream come to fruition. Setbacks and challenges seemed to loom around every corner, threatening to derail my aspirations. But through it all, I clung to a flicker of hope, trusting in the journey even when the path ahead seemed uncertain.

And then, in a twist of fate that I could never have predicted, the pieces began to fall into place. Opportunities arose where I least expected them, guiding me closer to my goal with each passing day. It was as if the universe itself had conspired to make my dream a reality, orchestrating a symphony of events that led me inexorably towards the cockpit of an airplane.

When the moment finally arrived, when I felt the exhilaration of flight coursing through my veins, it was a surreal experience beyond anything I had ever imagined. In that moment, I realized that life truly is a journey filled with unexpected surprises, and that sometimes, the most extraordinary dreams are realized in the most unlikely of ways.

Growing up, I witnessed firsthand the struggles of my parents as they fought against the tide of adversity to provide for our family. Their perseverance in the face of hardship left an indelible mark on my soul, teaching me the invaluable lesson that giving up is never an option, regardless of the challenges life may throw our way.

As I navigated through life, I encountered countless individuals who had resigned themselves to a fate dictated by circumstance. They spoke of dreams deferred and aspirations abandoned, citing age, family obligations, and a myriad of other excuses as reasons for their inertia. Yet, in their eyes, I saw a glimmer of regret, a silent acknowledgment of the paths not taken and the opportunities squandered.

But I refused to succumb to the same defeatist mindset. Inspired by the resilience of my parents, I resolved to forge my own path, determined to chase after my dreams with unwavering tenacity. For me, the prospect of settling for mediocrity was far more daunting than the prospect of facing hardships along the way.

Yes, the journey was arduous, fraught with obstacles and setbacks that threatened to derail my aspirations. But with each challenge, I drew strength from the example set by my parents, reminding myself that the struggle was a testament to my unwavering commitment to realizing my dreams.

And so, I pressed on, fueled by a burning desire to defy the odds and carve out a future defined by passion and purpose. For me, the choice was clear: I would rather endure the hardships of pursuing my dreams than live a life haunted by the specter of regret. And in the end, it was this unwavering resolve that propelled me towards the realization of my dreams, proving that age, family obligations, and adversity are but minor obstacles in the face of unyielding determination.

It's crucial to emphasize that while pursuing our dreams, we should never neglect our responsibilities towards our families and obligations. However, it's equally essential to recognize that we owe it to ourselves to nurture our own aspirations and ambitions. Striking a balance between our personal dreams and our familial duties is indeed a delicate tightrope to walk.

My message isn't about advocating for selfishness or disregarding the needs of others. Instead, it's about acknowledging that we have a duty to ourselves as well. Just as we devote ourselves to our loved ones and commitments, we must also prioritize our own growth and fulfillment. By doing so, we not only enrich our own lives but also become better equipped to contribute positively to the world around us.

So, to anyone who feels torn between their personal dreams and their familial responsibilities, I say this: don't give up. Push forward with determination and resilience, knowing that you have the capacity to achieve anything you set your mind to. By honoring your own aspirations while fulfilling your obligations, you'll discover a sense of fulfillment and purpose that enriches not only your own life but also the lives of those you hold dear to your heart.

The End

I DID IT, SO CAN YOU! – MAHENDRA JAGIR

www.ingramcontent.com/pod-product-compliance
Lightning Source LLC
Chambersburg PA
CBHW040805110726
47973CB00008B/108

* 9 7 9 8 3 3 0 2 4 3 3 9 6 *